The Graphic Art of Mary Cassatt

Organized by
THE MUSEUM OF GRAPHIC ART
New York

Participating Museums

Cincinnati Art Museum

The Cooper Union Museum, New York

Herron Museum of Art, Indianapolis

Museum of Fine Arts, Boston

National Collection of Fine Arts,

Smithsonian Institution

Philadelphia Museum of Art

The UCLA Art Galleries, University of California,

Los Angeles

1967-1968

The Graphic Art of Mary Cassatt

Introduction by
Adelyn D. Breeskin

Foreword by
Donald H. Karshan

The Museum of Graphic Art
and
Smithsonian Institution Press

*Published by The Museum of Graphic Art
and Smithsonian Institution Press.*

*Library of Congress Catalogue Card Number
67—30432.*

First printing 1967

*Designed and produced by Chanticleer Press, Inc.
Printed by Amilcare Pizzi S. p. A., Milano, Italy.*

Contents

Foreword

Descriptions of former exhibitions featuring prints by Mary Cassatt reveal that the present exhibition, organized by the Museum of Graphic Art, is by far the most extensive ever devoted to the artist's graphic work. With the exception of some varying states, the eighty prints and the three drawings in this exhibition are all reproduced in gravure and comprise Cassatt's most successful work in the graphic medium. Besides Mrs. Adelyn D. Breeskin's *catalogue raisonné* of 1948, this publication reproduces the largest number of her graphic works, including several prints and drawings previously undescribed, and is the fullest treatment of Cassatt's graphic art to date.

We were indeed fortunate to have Mrs. Breeskin, the foremost authority on Cassatt, as a special consultant to this exhibition, and as author of the introduction, chronology, catalogue, analysis of former exhibitions and bibliography.

The genius that was Mary Cassatt's flourished vividly in her prints. The reproductions in this publication, even though printed in gravure, can serve only as an introductory reference. One must behold the actual originals on museum walls, on print department study tables, or in the home, to appreciate fully their line, tone and color.

Two etchings by Edgar Degas (one is fig. 86), depicting Mary Cassatt, are included in the exhibition. By portraying her in the Louvre, Degas anticipated her later prominence and eventual representation in that museum. It is said that when Degas saw Cassatt's color aquatint, "Woman Bathing" (fig. 59), he asked, "That back, you modelled it?", and that Cassatt simply answered, "No." Achille Segard's explanation of this answer is illuminating: "Now in order to obtain that result, the artist did not even need to indicate shadow. That back curves by the sole power of the perfectly executed line. It has subtle precision, the more remarkable since that bit of mastery was obtained directly on copper without a preliminary design."[1] Claude Roger-Marx has written, "She may sometimes make us smile, but the last word always belongs to her fundamental good sense and, above all, her exquisite drawing."[2] Even Paul Gauguin was to say, "Mary Cassatt has charm, but she also has force."[3] These observations stand in opposition to critics of Cassatt's drawing. At her best, such as in the color prints, Cassatt displays a sureness and economy of line through which meaning and overall design take priority over mere virtuosity of figure drawing.

The exhibition of her recently completed color prints at Durand-Ruel in 1891 must have made a significant impression on many artists. Not since the 18th century in France had color aquatints been employed with such strength and total commitment. The subtle watercolor-like hues and flat patterns produced by the aquatint grain, working in harmony with linear patterns made by drypoint, created a new kind of visual excitement. In the 1890s color printing in Paris was dominated by lithography. Toulouse-Lautrec, Bonnard, Vuillard and others worked extensively in this medium. Although seldom acknowledged, it was most likely Cassatt's color

[1] Lemoisne, Vol. I, p. 191.
[2] Claude Roger-Marx, *Graphic Art: The 19th Century*, McGraw-Hill Book Co., Inc., New York, 1962, p. 166.
[3] Norman Schlenoff, *Encyclopedia of World Art*, McGraw-Hill Book Co., Inc., New York, 1960, Vol. III, p. 143.

prints that caused a limited revival of color aquatint printmaking. These prints probably influenced Jacques Villon to work in this medium, beginning in 1899. Aquatints such as "Autre Temps—1830" and "Cake-Walk des Petites Filles," both of 1904, show his indebtedness to Cassatt. Working in the revived tradition many years later, Georges Rouault applied his intense palette to further expand the color range of aquatint etching with his illustrations for the "Passion," in "Fleurs du Mal," and "Cirque," "Cirque de l'Etoile Filante" and in large aquatints such as "L'Automne." Cassatt emerges, then, as more than a 19th century figure in the graphic arts; her influence has been felt in printmaking of the present century.

Her art has also been criticized for its dominant mother and child theme, with its attendant "sentiment." Mrs. Breeskin points out in her introduction that this theme comprises less than one-third of Cassatt's graphic œuvre, which also underlines the fact that we need to see more of her prints. Nevertheless, it is interesting to delve into this response to her women and children. We may pose this question: why do we not tire of the themes that dominate the prints of several other artists: Toulouse-Lautrec's prostitutes, Degas' bathers, Matisse's odalisques or Picasso's satyrs? Can it be that these others seem more sophisticated because exotic, sensual or fanciful? Since few women have interpreted the maternal bond in the history of art, we may not be prepared to understand fully Cassatt's truly fresh and acute insights. Cassatt's interpretations of this subject, which penetrate children's personalities and maternal relationships, tend to be far less sentimental than similar portrayals by men. This exploration, of course, has a depth that emerges from Cassatt, the woman. Similarly, the delicacy, serenity and rarely-stated sense of privacy expressed in her color prints of feminine activities such as "Woman Bathing" (fig. 59), "The Fitting" (fig. 56), "The Letter" (fig. 55), also derive from Cassatt, the woman. The problem of appreciating her prints may require realization not only of her unique aesthetics, but also of her extraordinary sensitivity to female spirituality and the deepest of human ties—those between women and children. It is hoped that the present exhibition and catalogue will contribute to this realization.

With the Cassatt catalogue, the Museum of Graphic Art initiates a series of publications on important print-makers. Each of the Museum's future exhibitions of individual printmakers will be accompanied by a similar publication by a noted authority on that artist. The catalogues will be in a uniform format so that the publications will serve as a continuing set of volumes on graphic artists.

All of the many institutions and individuals who loaned works to this exhibition, including curators, collectors, and dealers, are to be thanked for their splendid cooperation. It is a testimony to the generous spirit of these lenders that they have allowed this exhibition to travel so extensively across the United States, thereby enabling a maximum number of persons to view Cassatt's full graphic range. Acknowledgment is due the trustees, staff and especially the print curators of the seven participating museums for their efforts and for the integration of the exhibition into their programs. Acknowledgment also should be made of the support of the Museum of Graphic Art's Board of Directors and its Founding Members. Thanks are due to Mourlot Imprimeurs of Paris for their work on the twelve-color lithographic poster for the exhibition, and to Chanticleer Press for the design and printing of this catalogue.

DONALD H. KARSHAN
President, The Museum of Graphic Art

Introduction

Since two very interesting and readable books have been published within the past year on the life of Mary Cassatt[1] it seems unnecessary to repeat once again the details of her remarkable career as one of the most important American artists of her time. This introduction will emphasize instead her work in the graphic processes together with related aspects of her art.

The fact that she was taken to live in Europe for seven years during her childhood was, in all likelihood, important in the formation of her determination to become an artist. At the age of sixteen she had already made this clear to her family and she was never swayed from her intended course until she was in France sketching in the Haute Savoie region, with her main base among family friends in Paris in 1867. The Franco-Prussian War forced her return to Philadelphia for about a year and a half, after which in 1872 she left for Parma, Italy, where she evidently started her training in printmaking.

At the local Academy, Carlo Raimondi (1809–1883) taught both painting and printmaking, and for eight months she worked with him, after which, in gratitude for his instruction, she presented him with an oil painting of the bust of a young woman which she inscribed "à mon ami C. Raimondi." No graphic work done by her under his tutelage seems to have survived, but when she took up the etching process again some years after settling in Paris in 1874, that earlier training must have helped her to familiarize herself with its various techniques.

While in Parma she concentrated also on the study of paintings by Correggio and also on those by Parmiganino. She was convinced that the best way to learn to paint was by studying works by the masters in museums rather than by instruction in an art school. She had already had three years at the Pennsylvania Academy which she had found insufficiently rewarding. The study of great paintings in museums, on the other hand, proved the most satisfactory means of learning for her, and she gained sufficient proficiency from such study so that when she sent a large painting entitled "On the Balcony" (now in the Philadelphia Museum) to the Paris Salon from Parma, which she painted while there, it was accepted.

The next year found her studying works by Velasquez and Rubens in Madrid and Seville, and from there she sent her second painting to the Salon, which was also accepted. To further her study of Rubens' work, she went to Antwerp and from there sent a painting to the Salon which showed much greater breadth of treatment, gained from her study of Rubens' work. It was a portrait head of Mme. Cortier (now in a private collection in New York City), entitled "Ida." When Degas went to see the Salon of 1873 he noted that portrait, studied it and commented, "That is true. There is someone who feels as I do."

Four years later, in 1877, a mutual friend, the artist Joseph Tourny, who had met Miss Cassatt in Belgium and had been with Degas when he first saw the painting of "Ida," brought him to Miss Cassatt to ask her to exhibit with a completely unheralded group, later called the Impressionists. Miss Cassatt reported to her friend

---

[1] Frederick A. Sweet, *Miss Mary Cassatt, Impressionist from Pennsylvania*, University of Oklahoma Press, Norman, 1966. Julia M. H. Carson, *Mary Cassatt*, David McKay, Inc., New York, 1966.

Mrs. H. O. Havemeyer, years later, how promptly she had accepted. And to her biographer Achille Segard she said, "At last, I could work with absolute independence without considering the opinion of a jury. I had already recognized who were my true masters. I admired Manet, Courbet and Degas. I hated conventional art—I began to live."

Thereafter she exhibited in four of the five Impressionist exhibitions and won not only favorable comments from critics such as Zola, Huysmans, and Mellerio but also the respect and friendship of the entire Impressionist group. Aside from her close associations with Degas, she became well acquainted with Manet, Morisot, Renoir, Monet, Pissarro, Guillaumin and made contact with Cézanne and Gauguin.

It was Degas who persuaded Miss Cassatt that to learn drawing she should draw on copper. She then told Segard that to impose on herself absolute precision in drawing after the living model, she chose this as a way of excluding all trickery and inexactitude. She was not satisfied to draw with a pencil; instead she chose to use metal and a steel point so that the plate would hold every trace of her mistakes or corrections. She insisted that it served as magnificent discipline and that there was none more severe, none which could give finer results.

In 1879 Degas wrote to his friend, the etcher Felix Bracquemond, about some prints that he, Pissarro and Cassatt were preparing for a journal, entitled *Le Jour et La Nuit* which he was planning to publish. He wrote, "The aquatint is progressing even without you (who should be teaching us instead of leaving us to our own devices)." And again, "We must talk about the journal. We have made some experiments. The one by Pissarro, for instance. Mlle. Cassatt is in the midst of some at this moment. It is impossible for me to do likewise to any extent, since I must earn a living . . . . Salmon (their printer) is rushing the work and will have all of the prints ready for Tuesday. I am eager to see them. I am greatly pleased with mine." And to Pissarro, Degas wrote, "Miss Cassatt is making some delightful graphic experiments. Come back soon. I am beginning to announce the Journal in different quarters."

The fact that the journal was never published seems regrettable to us. Nevertheless, it served a valuable purpose, not only in cementing a close friendship between Degas and Cassatt, but also in encouraging her to concentrate on the various graphic processes then and throughout her career. Her first few graphic works tabulated up to then were in etching, then came the one soft-ground on zinc, The Umbrella (fig. 2), and then a long series of soft-grounds with aquatint, plus one lithograph. The finest of these are of young women at the opera or "in the loge," one or two of which she prepared to show in the journal that was to have been launched by Degas in 1880.

The prints which Degas prepared for the journal were the two in which Mary Cassatt is seen from the rear, leaning on her umbrella. They were entitled, "Au Louvre: Musée des Antiques" (fig. 85) and "Au Louvre: La Peinture (Mary Cassatt)". Both were executed in etching, drypoint and aquatint whereas in the majority of the early prints Cassatt used soft-ground, rather than straight etching, with aquatint. This medium, which she gradually developed, was natural to her and was closely related to painting since, as she used it, it was largely a tonal process. However, for the most severe discipline, to develop precision in drawing from the living model, she soon found drypoint even more congenial and beneficial.

It was in the summer of 1880 that she began sketching her small nieces and nephew in drypoint, and although continuing her aquatints at the same time (developing such handsome, bold compositions as figs. 19, 20, 16, and 18), she worked most diligently in drypoint until she had completed the definitive series of twelve prints and one extra one entitled "Quietude" (fig. 45), all of which were first shown in her 1893 exhibition at Durand-Ruel's in Paris.

The series includes both studies of young women alone and of mothers with either a baby or a somewhat older little girl. These works of the mother and child theme should not be confused with the madonna type or the ideal mother of another world; they are instead very human mothers whose special, close relationship to their children is deeply felt, with a sense of protection and concern on the part of the mothers and of contentment and complete security on that of the babies. In these studies, for which she is best known but which actually comprise less than one third of her prints, she developed a feeling for individual character, natural charm and grace, for genuine sentiment as well as tenderness and harmonious accord. Since these infants and small children could not be expected to hold to any set pose for more than a minute or two they were a severe test of her draftsmanship, visual memory, and patience.

Her vision was definitely that of a realist. As she has commented, her true masters were Courbet, Manet, and Degas. In her painting style she actually accepted more from Manet than from Degas. Like Manet, she was only an Impressionist in the high key and luminosity of her palette and in her insistence on the importance of light as it plays on objects. She followed his advice to work outdoors, which she did increasingly throughout her career. And she was, even more consistently than either Manet or Degas, concerned primarily with the human figure. She was not a landscapist.

Degas' strongest influence on her was definitely his insistence on draftsmanship—the kind which she learned so thoroughly from her printmaking. Then, too, his sense of style and of composition influenced her strongly. In the soft-ground and aquatint entitled "In the Opera Box (No. 3)" (fig. 6), which she produced for his journal, one can see that she exerted her utmost to be worthy of being placed with him and Pissarro in this enterprise; the results must have given her definite satisfaction, especially since Degas praised the work highly. The pattern of the strong curve of the fan offset by the curves of the two balconies and the chandelier create an overall design that is both brilliant and stylish. Another one of her prints, very probably planned to be included in the journal, is "The Visitor" (fig. 7), which shows again a very definite influence of Degas. In his print "Au Louvre: Musée des Antiques" (fig. 85) we see the rear view of the standing figure of Miss Cassatt with her arm extended, leaning on an umbrella. This striking pose, with the sharp angle formed by the arm and the umbrella, catches the eye of the observer immediately. Miss Cassatt has used a similar device in "The Visitor" (fig. 7). In the pose of her standing figure, the arm outrstetched at an angle as she holds the back of a chair is the arresting point, leading the eye upward. The lighting effect in both prints is all-important. In the Degas it is more diffused and subtle; in the Cassatt simpler, but also very effective, the afternoon light through the high curtained window partly silhouetting the two figures. The comprehensive approach and spontaneous treatment is a further bond between these two works, which were executed while these two friends were working in close proximity during the early and formative years of Cassatt's career.

In addition to her work in soft-ground and aquatint and then in drypoint fully developed in the series of twelve prints for her exhibition in 1893, but actually created earlier, she added a unique graphic medium. The influence of Japanese prints was felt in Paris long before the big exhibition of 1890 held at the Ecole des Beaux-Arts, but that large exhibition, consisting of hundreds of prints, amazed Paris artists by its novelty, its originality and its completely different use of basic art concepts. Miss Cassatt went many times to see it—sometimes with Degas, again with her neighbor Berthe Morisot and her good friend, the poet Mallarmé.

Just as in earlier years she studied the art of painting by analyzing the works of Correggio and Rubens, so with the same intelligence and concentration she absorbed the art in these prints, especially the figure prints of Utamaro and Yeishi. She bought quite a number of them and hung them in her home for her constant enjoyment. The series of ten color prints which followed marked one of her greatest triumphs and one which would give her just claim to fame even if they were her sole accomplishment. They not only added a new chapter to the history of printmaking but, to my mind, have to this day never been surpassed.

After her thorough study of those Japanese prints, which were woodblock prints done in a technique quite alien to her, she had to think of a way of translating them into her own particular vision. And this she succeeded in doing quite marvellously. She described the process in a letter to Mr. Frank Weitenkampf, then Curator of Prints at the New York Public Library: "I drew the outlines in drypoint and laid on a ground where color was to be applied, then colored "à la poupée.' [This means that she applied her color with little 'dolls,' or rags twisted over conically pointed sticks.] I was entirely ignorant of the method when I began and as all the plates were colored by me, I varied sometimes the manner of applying the color. The set of ten plates was done with the intention of attempting an imitation of Japanese methods. Of course I abandoned that somewhat after the first plate and tried more for atmosphere."

It is interesting that she failed to mention the use of soft-ground in this written description of the process. A number of the preparatory drawings still exist, however, which were used for applying the soft-ground lines onto the plates. The artist Sue Fuller was the first to notice this technical detail and published an article in which she also insists that Miss Cassatt used soft-ground rather than aquatint for the base of many of her color areas.[2]

In a letter to the collector Mr. Samuel P. Avery, written in 1903, preserved in the New York Public Library, Miss Cassatt wrote, "It is delightful to think that you take an interest in my work. I have sent with the set of my coloured etchings all the 'states' I have. I wish I could have had more, but I had to hurry on and be ready for my printer when I could get him. The printing is a great work; sometimes we worked all day (eight hours) both, as hard as we could work and only printed eight or ten proofs in a day. My method is very simple. I drew an outline in drypoint and transferred this to two other plates, making in all three plates, never more, for each proof. Then I put on aquatint wherever the color was to be printed; the color was painted on the plate as it was to appear in the proof." Running these large plates through the press was a laborious job and to do this for the set of ten she had the assistance of the printer, LeRoy. She very generously included his name on the signature: "Imprimé par l'artiste et M. LeRoy."

The process used may be further described thus: first a pencil sketch was drawn of the composition on paper. This was then placed over a copper plate covered (in most cases) with soft-ground, and the main outlines were re-drawn, the soft-ground adhering to the paper wherever a line was re-drawn. The outlines were then bitten in soft-ground very lightly and then re-drawn in drypoint. These steps were repeated on two other plates of about the same dimensions. The areas of aquatint were next applied, different areas on each of the three plates, so that no two areas when printed in colors would run together. Careful planning of color areas is the secret of Miss Cassatt's supreme clarity and brilliance in color printing. In planning her designs for patterned dresses, for instance, the background color was printed from one plate, the pattern from one or both of the others. The pattern could appear on the key (or outline) plate, but the background dress color could not or it would run into the outlines.

The aquatint was of the finest grain, expertly applied. Some trial proofs have been found in which the aquatint for flesh tones was printed a solid black, after which it was scraped down to a very light tint. Since the prints were colored by the artist "à la poupée," the amount of ink helped to determine the density of tone. Therefore each impression of these prints differs slightly from every other one. Some impressions are more intensely colored than others. Also the actual color used is sometimes varied. As in her black and white drypoints, the burr soon wore down so that earlier impressions (in the edition of twenty-five) show more delicate lines and more rich black lines, which wore away before the end of the edition. Many of the lines were reinforced during the course of the taking of the trial proofs, some also during the run of the edition but even so, by the end of the edition, they were visibly weakened.

---

[2] See her very interesting article, "Mary Cassatt's Use of Soft-Ground Etching," *Magazine of Art*, pp. 54–57, February, 1950. Her interpretations of the soft-ground techniques used in Br. 27, 34, and 107 are most revealing and show that Miss Cassatt was revolutionary in her use of soft-ground.

The set of the ten color prints impressed Pissarro to such an extent that he wrote in 1891 to his son Lucien, in London, "It is absolutely necessary, while what I saw yesterday at Miss Cassatt's is still fresh in mind, to tell you about the colored engravings she is to show at Durand-Ruel's at the same time as I. We open Saturday, the same day as the patriots who, between the two of us, are going to be furious when they discover right next to their exhibition a show of rare and exquisite works.

"You remember the effects you strove for at Eragny? Well, Miss Cassatt has realized just such effects, and admirably; the tone even, subtle, delicate, without stains or seams, adorable blues, fresh rose, etc. Then what must we have to succeed?—money, yes, just a little money. We have to have copper plates, a *boîte à grain*, this was a bit of a nuisance but it is absolutely necessary to have uniform and imperceptible grains and a good printer. But the result is admirable, as beautiful as Japanese work, and it's done with printer's ink. When I get some prints I will send you some; incidentally I have agreed to do a series with Miss Cassatt; I will do some Markets, Peasant Women in the Fields and—this is really wonderful—I will be able to try to put to the proof some of the principles of neo-impressionism. What do you think? If we could make some beautiful engravings, that would really be something.

"I have seen attempts at color engraving which will appear in the exhibition of the patriots, but the work is ugly, heavy, lusterless and commercial. I am sure that Miss Cassatt's effort will be taken up by all the tricksters who will make empty and pretty things. We have to act before the idea is seized by people without aesthetic principle."

However, these color prints have remained quite unique and rank with Cassatt's finest paintings and pastels as among her major works. After they were shown in this first exhibition in Paris, Pissarro wrote again to Lucien, "What has befallen Miss Cassatt is just what I predicted: great indifference on the part of the visitors and even much opposition." Degas, however, was flattering. He was charmed by the noble element in her work and upon viewing the "Woman Bathing" (fig. 59) he commented that he would not admit that a woman was able to draw that well! Such draftsmanship is indeed masterly, and it was evidently done directly from the model on the copper without preliminary sketches. At least none has so far been found. The viewpoint is from a low level, an angle which was very popular with Japanese printmakers. The boldly striped robe, dropped below the waist, the patterned rug and the well-drawn pitcher in the left foreground are also seen under that influence. Even the describing of the washstand, with its simple ruled lines for moldings, is similar to their treatment of furniture accessories.

Throughout the entire series such influences abound, but they were assimilated into her own style so that she thus enlarged its scope and added stature to her art. With her superior intelligence and taste she retained the very best that she had already achieved and added to it what she well understood and knew how to use for the good of her art. The painting in the Art Institute of Chicago entitled "The Bath," done at about the same time as the prints, shows her use of this new enlargement of her style in the oil medium. It is among her most important paintings.

Aside from her color prints and the series of twelve drypoints, her work in the print field was largely undertaken just as exercise to perfect her drawing, and many of her prints are free, fresh, spontaneous essays, quite lacking the usual conventional detail and finish. She never listed them, never entitled or dated them with any accuracy and often signed them years after they were done, meanwhile forgetting the number and order of states. Consequently we find that she would sometimes write "*épreuve d'essai*" on a finished state. She was accustomed to place her stamp (the interlaced M and C), usually in blue ink, on the finished states of prints which she had approved. But even in this procedure she was not consistent, as the stamp appears on some trial proofs and is absent from some satisfactory prints of finished states.

She sold comparatively few prints; the majority of them therefore exist only in a small series of proofs and were not printed for sale. Those which were exhibited at Durand-Ruel's, including the fine series of twelve drypoints and the color prints, were published in editions of twenty-five impressions. About four other plates were supposedly printed in an edition of fifty, but it is quite likely that the number remained incomplete.

In 1923, three years before Miss Cassatt's death, her companion-maid, Mathilde Vallet, found twenty-five plates in a closet. They were all drypoints except two, and Miss Cassatt, then practically blind, was told that they had never been printed. They were shown to her printer, Delâtre, who then proceeded to print each of the twenty-five in an edition of nine prints. Of the nine, one set of these twenty-five prints was sent to Mrs. Havemeyer to show to Mr. William M. Ivins, Jr., Curator of Prints at the Metropolitan Museum, with a request that he might exhibit them and if the museum wished to buy a set the price was to be $ 2,000. Mr. Ivins actually sent photographs to Miss Cassatt to prove that they all had been printed before and suggested therefore that each of the restrikes should be marked with the date 1923. When the photographs were shown to Delâtre, he said, "What does this prove? I know there may be one or even two proofs of them, but I defy them to show a series." Actually, aside from the two series of the color prints and of the twelve drypoints, with the other four above mentioned, published supposedly in an edition of fifty, very few of Miss Cassatt's prints were printed in more than a few proofs. Therefore, Mr. Ivins was correct in his suggestion that these restrikes be dated to show that they were just that. But Miss Cassatt refused to do so and was made so angry that she never forgave her friend Mrs. Havemeyer, nor Mr. Ivins.

The quality of the restrikes is not equal to that of Miss Cassatt's best work. She was very particular about the printing of her plates and would accept only clear, rich impressions. Certainly, if she had retained her eyesight she would have been the first to criticize the lack of sharpness and evenness of line in the reprints. She refused to sign the proofs 1923, but she decided, due to Mr. Ivins opinion concerning them, not to sell them. They have come on the market only since her death.

It is also important to mention the recent publishing of a very close facsimile of the transfer lithograph "Sara Wearing her Bonnet and Coat" (fig. 82), which is being placed on the market as an original by Miss Cassatt. We exhibit it in this exhibition together with an original print to point out the differences.

The series of ten color prints together with two more of them (figs. 64 and 65) were included in her much larger 1893 Paris exhibition and after two more years they were exhibited in New York. But very few of them were sold and Miss Cassatt wrote to her dealers, Durand-Ruel, "I am still very much disappointed that my compatriots have so little liking for any of my work." Nevertheless she persevered, adding five more color prints to enhance her triumph in the creation of these beautiful and now exceedingly rare prints, which rank among her very finest works.

In considering Miss Cassatt's art as a whole we find that she was tremendously industrious, working throughout her formative period and the time of the full flowering of her talents with such concentrated activity that together with at least 225 prints she left about three hundred oil paintings and four hundred pastels, not to mention watercolors and drawings. A fair proportion of these many works were done after her return from her one lengthy trip home to America in 1898–99 when she first felt the urge to help the Havemeyers and a number of other friends and relatives in buying fine paintings and thus bringing more great works of art to our shores. In taking on this assignment, she allowed her own work to have a less dominant place in her life.

Consequently we can mark off four distinct periods of her production, namely the student years of 1869–1879, the very revealing formative years from 1879 to 1888, the brilliant years of preparation for her first exhibitions and the stimulating years that followed (from 1888 to 1898) and then, after her trip to America, the tapering off of her best efforts until she finally stopped working in 1914. This schedule was somewhat abbreviated for her work in the print field, since she seems to have started concentrating on her printmaking only in 1879 and she was forced to stop working on metal in 1910 because her eyes were beginning to bother her and the shine of the copper hurt them. Her last prints were mere starts—tragic failures due to the progressive blindness which stopped all of her work in 1914. She then had to live on until her death all of twelve years later, without her work and without her eyesight.

Her art remains to perpetuate the memory of a remarkable woman who achieved a place for herself as the only American within the Impressionist group. Although transplanted to French soil, she retained her own native personality. At the same time, together with Degas, she upheld the precepts of the mainstream of French art with its great respect for the classic viewpoint. At her best, which includes many of the prints in this exhibition, she ranks as an artist worthy of the great renown which she has only very recently won.

ADELYN D. BREESKIN

Biographical Chronology

1844	Born, May 22, Allegheny City, Pennsylvania (now a part of Pittsburgh)—the third child of Mr. and Mrs. Robert S. Cassatt.
1851–1858	Lives with her family in Paris, Heidelberg and Darmstadt.
1858–1868	Lives with her family in Philadelphia.
1861–1865	Studies at the Pennsylvania Academy of Fine Arts.
1867	Goes to France with another Academy student to sketch and paint.
1870–1871	Returns to Philadelphia because of the Franco-Prussian War.
1872	Goes to Parma, Italy, and studies at the Academy with Carlo Raimondi (1809–1883), who teaches her graphic techniques. Also concentrates on the study of the paintings of Correggio and Parmigianino in Parma. Sends her first painting, "On the Balcony," to the Paris Salon.
1873	Goes to Seville, from where she sends her second painting to the Salon, and then on to Belgium and Holland and finally to Paris again.
1874	Sends her third painting, "Portrait of Mme. Cortier," to the Salon. Visits Rome and sends her first two Salon paintings to the National Academy of Design in New York.
1877	Her parents and her older sister, Lydia, come to Paris to live with her. Degas invites her to join the Impressionists.
1879	Sends her first two Impressionist paintings to the Society of American Artists—probably the first of her paintings shown in America.

1879–1880	Works very hard preparing prints for *Le Jour et La Nuit*, a journal that Degas planned but never published.
1879, 1880, 1881, 1886	Exhibits paintings in the fourth, fifth, sixth and eighth Impressionist Exhibitions.
1880	Her brother Alexander Cassatt brings his family for a visit and she charms his children into posing for her.
1882	Her sister Lydia dies.
1887	The family moves to the apartment and studio at 10 rue Marignan, which she keeps for the rest of her life.
1890	Visits the great Japanese print exhibition at the Ecole des Beaux-Arts in Paris.
1890–1891	For the summer and fall she rents Château Bachivillers on the Oise, sets up her etching press and works on the set of ten color prints with the help of the printer LeRoy.
1891	On June 10, has her first one-man show at Durand-Ruel's, including the set of ten color prints as well as two oils and two pastels. Her father dies.
1892	Mrs. Potter Palmer commissions her to do a large mural for the Woman's Building of the World's Columbian Exposition at Chicago. She completes it at Château Bachivillers. Unfortunately it is destroyed after the exposition closes.
1893	A larger one-man show at Durand-Ruel's containing ninety-eight items. She buys the Château Beaufresne, at Mesnil-Theribus, Oise, her summer home for the rest of her life.
1895	Her mother dies.
1898–1899	Her first visit back to America since settling in Paris in 1874. She visits her brothers outside of Philadelphia, the Havemeyers and Stillmans in New York, the Whittemores in Naugatuck and the Hammonds in Boston.

1901	Accompanies the Havemeyers to Italy and Spain and encourages them to buy El Grecos and other great paintings that were later given to the Metropolitan Museum of Art.
1904	Made a Chevalier of the Legion of Honor.
1905	Competes for a mural for the new capitol at Harrisburg, Pennsylvania, but withdraws upon hearing of graft.
1906	Death of her brother Alexander, formerly president of the Pennsylvania Railroad.
1908–1909	Last visit to America.
1910–1911	Stops working on her drypoints because the shine of the copper hurts her eyes. Goes to Egypt with her brother Gardner Cassatt and his family.
1911–1912	Nervous breakdown and illness after brother Gardner's death.
1912	First operation for cataracts on both eyes.
1914	Awarded Gold Medal of Honor by Pennsylvania Academy. Stops painting due to progressive blindness.
1914–1918	During First World War spends most of the time in Grasse, on the Riviera.
1926	Dies at Château Beaufresne on June 14.

Cassatt Exhibitions Featuring Prints

April 1891
Galerie Durand-Ruel, Paris

The series of 10 color prints, together with two oils and two pastels.

November-December, 1893
Galerie Durand-Ruel, Paris

The series of 10 color prints with two additional color prints, i. e., "The Banjo Lesson" (Br. 156), "Gathering Fruit" ·[also called "Le Potager" (Br. 157)], the series of 12 drypoints plus 15 early soft-ground and aquatints, other drypoints and the early lithograph. With these were shown 17 oils and 14 pastels.

April 16—30, 1895
Galerie Durand-Ruel, New York

The series of 10 color prints, "The Banjo Lesson" (Br. 156), "Gathering Fruit" (Br. 157), "Peasant Mother and Child" (Br. 159), the series of 12 drypoints and "Gardner Held by his Mother" (Br. 113), and "Quietude" (Br. 139).

March 24—April 15, 1908
Galerie Vollard, Paris

A group of color prints plus drypoints together with 37 pastels and 13 oils.

June 8—27, 1914
Galerie Durand-Ruel, Paris

Four color prints, i. e., "The Banjo Lesson" (Br. 156), "Peasant Mother and Child" (Br. 159), "By the Pond" (Br. 161), and "The Barefooted Child" (Br. 160). The series of 12 drypoints, both lithographs and 37 other prints together with 12 oils and 17 pastels.

April 5—20, 1915
Galerie Durand-Ruel, New York

The series of 10 color prints plus "Peasant Mother and Child" (Br. 159), "The Barefooted Child" (Br. 160), "Gathering Fruit" (Br. 157), and "Under the Horse Chestnut Tree" (Br. 162), the series of 12 drypoints, and 33 other drypoints.

December 21, 1926—January 24, 1927
Art Institute, Chicago

The set of 10 color prints, plus 17 paintings, and pastels.

March 15—April 15, 1928 Carnegie Institute, Pittsburgh	The series of 10 color prints, "Feeding the Ducks" (Br. 158), "Peasant Mother and Child" (Br. 159), two states of color print "By the Pond" (Br. 161), plus "Gathering Fruit" (Br. 157), "Under the Horse Chestnut Tree" (Br. 162), "On the Balcony" (Br. 120), "Portrait of the Artist's Mother" (Br. 122), 11 drypoints and 13 aquatints.
March 10—November 2, 1930 The H. O. Havemeyer Coll. Metropolitan Museum of Art, New York	"Peasant Mother and Child" (Br. 159), "Feeding the Ducks" (Br. 158), "The Barefooted Child" (Br. 160), and "Under the Horse Chestnut Tree" (Br. 162). The series of 12 drypoints and 4 other drypoints, plus 2 oils and 2 pastels.
January 7—February 10, 1936 Baltimore Museum of Art	The series of 10 color prints in various states plus "The Banjo Lesson" (Br. 156), "By the Pond" (Br. 161), "The Barefooted Child" (Br. 160), "Under the Horse Chestnut Tree" (Br. 162), the series of 10 drypoints, a few later drypoints, the early lithograph, together with a few oils, pastels, watercolors and drawings.
May 13—June 10, 1939 Haverford College, Haverford, Pa.	Seven from the series of 10 color prints, "The Banjo Lesson" (Br. 156), "By the Pond" (Br. 161), "Under the Horse Chestnut Tree" (Br. 162), and 15 drypoints, plus 30 oils and pastels.
November 19—December 27, 1939 New Jersey State Museum Trenton, New Jersey	The series of 10 color prints, 3 trial proofs "Peasant Mother and Child" (Br. 159), "The Banjo Lesson" (Br. 156), the series of 12 drypoints plus an assortment of later drypoints and some earlier ones. Also 6 oils and 5 pastels.
November 28—January 11, 1941—1942 Baltimore Museum of Art	The series of 10 color prints, "The Banjo Lesson" (Br. 156), "Gathering Fruit" (Br. 157), "Feeding the Ducks" (Br. 158), "Peasant Mother and Child" (Br. 159), "The Barefooted Child" (Br. 160), "By the Pond" (Br. 161), "Under the Horse Chestnut Tree" (Br. 162), "The Portrait of the Artist's Mother" (Br. 122), the set of 12 drypoints plus a cross-section of others of her prints, 76 prints altogether as well as 63 oils and pastels, 3 watercolors, and 13 drawings.

June 12—through summer, 1946 Brooklyn Museum, Brooklyn	Five of the set of 10 color prints, the "Banjo Lesson" (Br. 156), and "By the Pond" (Br. 161), 3 of the set of 12 drypoints, the transfer lithograph and 3 other drypoints.
October 29—December 6, 1947 Wildenstein and Co., New York	Seven of the series of 10 color prints and the 7 which followed them. The set of 12 drypoints, the early lithograph and 5 early soft-ground and aquatints and 5 later drypoints as well as 49 oils and pastels.
October 1951 Pasadena Art Institute, Pasadena, Calif. "Mary Cassatt and her Parisian Friends"	Nine of the series of 10 color prints, "Gathering Fruit" (Br. 157), "Peasant Mother and Child" (Br. 159), 6 of the series of 12 drypoints, plus 7 soft-ground and aquatints, 3 drypoints, 9 oils, 3 pastels, and 6 drawings.
January 14—February 25, 1954 March 25—May 23, 1954 Art Institute of Chicago and Metropolitan Museum of Art, New York, "Sargent, Whistler, and Mary Cassatt"	The set of 10 color prints, together with 27 oils and pastels.
1955, Pennsylvania Academy at Peale House Gallery, Philadelphia, Pa.	Four states of "Under the Horse Chestnut Tree" (Br. 162), "The Fitting" (Br. 147), "Afternoon Tea Party" (Br. 151), "Woman Bathing" (Br. 148), "The Banjo Lesson" (Br. 156), 10 drypoints from the series of 12, 8 other drypoints, 7 oils, 3 pastels, and 1 watercolor.
April 22—May 29, 1960 Philadelphia Museum of Art	The series of 10 color prints, "The Banjo Lesson" (Br. 156), "The Barefooted Child" (Br. 160), "By the Pond" (Br. 161), "Under the Horse Chestnut Tree" (Br. 162), 8 of the series of 12 drypoints, 5 early soft-ground and aquatints, 15 other drypoints and the transfer lithograph together with 24 oils, 19 pastels, and 2 drawings.
November 25—January 10, 1960 Centre Culturel Americain, Paris	Nine of the set of 10 color prints [all but "The Lamp" (Br. 144)] and "The Banjo Lesson" (Br. 156), five from the series of 12 drypoints, "Quietude" (Br. 139), 8 later drypoints, 1 monotype, 8 soft-ground and aquatints, 5 oils, 1 watercolor, and 5 pastels.

April 18—June 3, 1962
Baltimore Museum of Art
"Manet, Degas, Berthe Morisot and
Mary Cassatt"

Seven of the series of 10 color prints, "By the Pond" (Br. 161), 4 of the series of 12 drypoints, 2 lithographs, "In the Opera Box No. 3" (Br. 22), 12 oils, 5 pastels, 10 drawings, and 1 watercolor.

June—July, 1965
Château de Beaufresne, Musée
Departemental de L'Oise-Beauvais
"Hommage à Mary Cassatt"

Eight of the series of 10 color prints, "The Banjo Lesson" (Br. 156), "Feeding the Ducks" (Br. 158), 3 of the series of 12 drypoints, "Quietude" (Br. 139), 9 other drypoints, 3 soft-ground and aquatints, 2 oils, 1 watercolor and 1 drawing.

November—December, 1965
International Galleries, Chicago
"Mary Cassatt"

"The Barefooted Child" (Br. 160), "By the Pond" (Br. 161), 3 of the series of 12 drypoints (Br. 129, 130, 136), 15 other drypoints, 22 soft-ground and aquatints, 3 oils, 4 pastels, 8 drawings, 2 watercolors.

July 30—August 20, 1967
Parrish Art Museum
Southampton, New York

The series of 10 color prints plus "Peasant Mother and Child" (Br. 159), "The Banjo Lesson" (Br. 156); "By the Pond" (Br. 161), "Under the Horse Chestnut Tree" (Br. 162), four of the series of 12 drypoints plus 7 other prints with 13 oils, 8 pastels, and 2 drawings.

Lenders to the Exhibition

Achenbach Foundation for Graphic Arts,
San Francisco
The Art Institute of Chicago
The Brooklyn Museum
Carnegie Institute, Pittsburgh
Cincinnati Art Museum
The Cooper Union Museum, New York
The Library of Congress, Washington, D. C.
Lucas Collection: c/o Baltimore Museum of Art
The Metropolitan Museum of Art, New York
The Minneapolis Institute of Arts
The Museum of Modern Art, New York
National Gallery of Art (Rosenwald Collection),
Washington, D. C.
The New York Public Library (S. P. Avery
Collection)
Philadelphia Museum of Art

Mrs. Gardner Cassatt, Bryn Mawr
International Galleries, Chicago
Miss Geraldine Johnson, Paris
Kovler Gallery: Chicago
Mr. and Mrs. John Palmer Leeper, San Antonio
Mrs. Percy C. Madeira, Berwyn, Pa.
Martin Gallery, New York
Mr. Samuel H. Nowak, Philadelphia
Mrs. Robert Penn, Chicago
M. Henri M. Petiet, Paris
Mrs. Lee C. Schlesinger, Metairie, La.
Mr. and Mrs. Daniel H. Silberberg, New York
Mr. Carl Zigrosser, Philadelphia

Catalogue

Note: Measurements are given in inches. Height precedes width.
"Br." numbers refer to Breeskin catalogue designations from The Graphic Work of Mary Cassatt,
A Catalogue Raisonné *by Adelyn D. Breeskin, H. Bittner and Company, 1948.*

1 Waiting   c. 1880
soft-ground and aquatint, $8^1/_2 \times 5^3/_4$
(Br. 11)   undescribed state between 3rd and
final state
M. Henri M. Petiet

2 The Umbrella   1879
soft-ground on zinc, $10^7/_8 \times 7^5/_{16}$
(Br. 5)   1st of two states
M. Henri M. Petiet

3 The Corner of the Sofa (No. 3)   c. 1880
soft-ground and aquatint, $8^1/_8 \times 6^5/_{16}$
(Br. 16)   3rd and final state
The Art Institute of Chicago

4 The Corner of the Sofa (No. 1)   c. 1880
drawing for soft-ground etching (Br. 14)
$11 \times 8^1/_4$
The Art Institute of Chicago

5 Two Young Ladies, Seated in a Loge, Facing
Right   c. 1880
soft-ground, aquatint and drypoint, $10^7/_8 \times 8^9/_{16}$
(Br. 18) 1st of two states
New York Public Library, Courtesy of the S. P.
Avery Collection. Astor, Lenox and Tilden
Foundations

6 In the Opera Box (No. 3)   c. 1880
soft-ground and aquatint, $8^1/_{16} \times 7^1/_4$
(Br. 22)   3rd and final state
Lucas Collection: c/o Baltimore Museum of Art

7 The Visitor   c. 1880
soft-ground, aquatint and drypoint $15^5/_8 \times 12^3/_{16}$
(Br. 34)   5th and final state
National Gallery of Art (Rosenwald Collection)

8 Heads of Elsie and Robert Cassatt   1880
drypoint, $4^{13}/_{16} \times 3^7/_8$
(Br. 38)   1st of two states
M. Henri M. Petiet

9 Mrs. Cassatt Reading to her Grandchildren
(No. 1)   1880
soft-ground, aquatint and drypoint, $6^1/_8 \times 11^3/_4$
(Br. 58)   4th and final state
M. Henri M. Petiet

10 Woman Seated in a Loge   c. 1881
lithograph on stone, $11^3/_8 \times 8^3/_4$
(Br. 23)   2nd and final state
Lucas Collection: c/o Baltimore Museum of Art

11 Lady in Black, in a Loge, Facing Right   c. 1881
soft-ground and aquatint, $7^5/_8 \times 11^5/_8$
(Br. 24)   2nd of three states
Lucas Collection: c/o Baltimore Museum of Art

12 George Moore   c. 1881
soft-ground and aquatint, $8^3/_4 \times 5^1/_2$
(Br. 27)   1st of three states
M. Henri M. Petiet

13 Knitting in the Glow of a Lamp   c. 1881
soft-ground, aquatint and etching, $11^5/_{16} \times 9$
(Br. 31)   only known state
M. Henri M. Petiet

14 Knitting in the Library   c. 1881
soft-ground and aquatint, $10^7/_8 \times 8^9/_{16}$
(Br. 30)   2nd state (restrike, 1923)
Mrs. Robert Penn

15 Lydia at Afternoon Tea   c. 1881
soft-ground and aquatint, $5^1/_2 \times 7^{13}/_{16}$
(Br. 68)   4th and final state
National Gallery of Art (Rosenwald Collection)

16 Lydia and her Mother at Tea   c. 1881
soft-ground and aquatint, 7×11
(Br. 69)   4th of five states
National Gallery of Art (Rosenwald Collection)

17 Under the Lamp   c. 1881
drawing for soft-ground and aquatint, $8 \times 8^1/_2$
(Br. 71)
Mr. Samuel H. Nowak

18 Under the Lamp   c. 1881
soft-ground and aquatint, $7^3/_4 \times 8^{11}/_{16}$
(Br. 71)   1st of two states
New York Public Library, Courtesy of the
S. P. Avery Collection. Astor, Lenox and Tilden
Foundations

19 Before the Fireplace (No. 1)   c. 1881
soft-ground and aquatint, $6^7/_{16} \times 8^1/_{16}$
(Br. 64)   3rd and final state
Mrs. Percy C. Madeira

20 Before the Fireplace (No. 2)   c. 1881
soft-ground and aquatint, $6^1/_4 \times 8^5/_8$
(Br. 65)   only known state
Ex-coll. Roger-Marx
Mr. Carl Zigrosser

21 Reading the Newspaper (No. 2)   c. 1883
soft-ground and aquatint, $5^3/_8 \times 6^1/_2$
(Br. 73)   3rd and final state
The Art Institute of Chicago

22 Mr. Cassatt Reading   c. 1883
soft-ground and aquatint, $6^9/_{16} \times 4^{15}/_{16}$
(Br. 74)   only known state
M. Henri M. Petiet

23 Mrs. Cassatt Knitting, Profile View   c. 1883
soft-ground and aquatint, $5^{11}/_{16} \times 4^5/_{16}$
(Br. 75)   only known state
Ex-coll. A. Barrion
The Library of Congress

24 Susan and Child Facing Each Other   c. 1883
etching and drypoint, $5^3/_8 \times 5$
(Br. 46)   only known state
The Cooper Union Museum

25 Mlle. Luguet Seated on a Couch   c 1883
soft-ground and aquatint, $8^1/_2 \times 5^1/_2$
(Br. 49)   2nd and final state
Miss Geraldine Johnson

26 Mlle. Luguet in a Coat and Hat   c. 1883
soft-ground, $8^1/_2 \times 5$
(Br. 48)   only known state
The Minneapolis Institute of Arts

27 Susan Seated before a Row of Trees   c. 1883
etching and drypoint, $9^3/_{16} \times 6^1/_2$
(Br. 54)   only known state
M. Henri M. Petiet

28 Robert Seated, Facing Left   1885
drypoint, $6^1/_4 \times 4^5/_8$
(Br. 82)   only known state
Metropolitan Museum of Art, Gift of Mrs. Imrie
de Vegh

29 Solicitude   c. 1889
drypoint, $7^3/_8 \times 5^7/_8$
(Br. 102)   4th and final state
International Galleries, Chicago

30 Nurse and Baby Bill (No. 2)   c. 1889
soft-ground and aquatint, $8^1/_2 \times 5^3/_8$
(Br. 109)   2nd and final state
Lucas Collection: c/o Baltimore Museum of Art

31 On the Balcony   c. 1889
soft-ground and aquatint, $10^7/_8 \times 8^1/_2$
(Br. 120)   2nd of three states
Cincinnati Art Museum

32 A Portrait of the Artist's Mother   c. 1889
soft-ground and aquatint, $9^7/_8 \times 7^1/_{16}$
(Br. 122)   undescribed state after the 6th state
Carnegie Institute

33 Baby's Back 1890
drypoint, $9^3/_{16} \times 6^7/_{16}$
(Br. 128) 3rd and final state
New York Public Library, Courtesy of the
S. P. Avery Collection. Astor, Lenox and Tilden
Foundations

34 The Map (also called The Lesson) 1890
drypoint, $6^1/_4 \times 9^3/_{16}$
(Br. 127) 3rd and final state
Lucas Collection: c/o Baltimore Museum of Art

35 The Mandolin Player 1889
drypoint, $9^5/_{16} \times 6^3/_{16}$
(Br. 130) 4th of seven states
The Library of Congress

36 The Stocking 1890
drypoint, $10^1/_{16} \times 7^3/_8$
(Br. 129) 5th of six states
Lucas Collection: c/o Baltimore Museum of Art

37 Repose 1890
drypoint, $9^1/_4 \times 6^9/_{16}$
(Br. 132) 4th and final state
The Art Institute of Chicago

38 Reflection c. 1890
drypoint, $10^3/_{16} \times 6^5/_{16}$
(Br. 131) 5th and final state
The Library of Congress

39 Tea 1890
drypoint, $7 \times 6^1/_8$
(Br. 133) 5th and final state
The Library of Congress

40 Nursing c. 1891
drypoint, $9^5/_8 \times 7$
(Br. 135) 3rd and final state
The Art Institute of Chicago

41 The Mirror 1891
drypoint, $8^7/_8 \times 6^{11}/_{16}$
(Br. 136) 6th and final state
New York Public Library, Courtesy of the
S. P. Avery Collection. Astor, Lenox and Tilden
Foundations

42 The Bonnet 1891
drypoint, $7^1/_4 \times 5^7/_{16}$
(Br. 137) 3rd and final state
Metropolitan Museum of Art, Gift of
Mrs. Gustavus S. Wallace

43 The Parrot 1891
drypoint, $6^3/_8 \times 4^{11}/_{16}$
(Br. 138) 3rd of seven states, $6^1/_4 \times 4^{11}/_{16}$
The Minneapolis Institute of Arts

44 The Parrot 1891
drypoint, $6^3/_8 \times 4^{11}/_{16}$
(Br. 138) 7th and final state
The Art Institute of Chicago

45 Quietude 1891
drypoint, $10^1/_4 \times 6^5/_8$
(Br. 139) 5th and final state
Lucas Collection: c/o Baltimore Museum of Art

46 Mrs. Gardner Cassatt and her Baby Seated
Near a Window 1891
drypoint, $8^5/_{16} \times 5^7/_{16}$
(Br. 112) only known state
New York Public Library, Courtesy of the
S. P. Avery Collection. Astor, Lenox and Tilden
Foundations

47 Gardner Held by his Mother 1891
drypoint, $8^5/_{16} \times 5^1/_2$
(Br. 113) only known state
Lucas Collection: c/o Baltimore Museum of Art

48 The Caress 1891
drypoint, $7^3/_4 \times 5^3/_4$
(Br. 140) 5th and final state
M. Henri M. Petiet

49 The Bath (also called The Tub) 1891
color print, with drypoint, soft-ground and
aquatint, $12^5/_{16} \times 9^{13}/_{16}$
(Br. 143) 5th of eleven states
National Gallery of Art (Rosenwald Collection)

50 The Bath (also called The Tub) 1891
color print with drypoint, soft-ground and
aquatint, $12^5/_{16} \times 9^{13}/_{16}$
(Br. 143) 6th of eleven states
National Gallery of Art (Rosenwald Collection)

51 The Bath (also called The Tub) 1891
color print, with drypoint, soft-ground and
aquatint, $12^5/_{16} \times 9^{13}/_{16}$
(Br. 143) 10th of eleven states
National Gallery of Art (Rosenwald Collection)

52 The Bath (also called The Tub) 1891
color print with drypoint, soft-ground and
aquatint, $12^5/_{16} \times 9^{13}/_{16}$
(Br. 143) 11th and final state
Private collection

53 In the Omnibus (also called The Tramway)
1891
color print, with drypoint, soft-ground and
aquatint, $14^1/_2 \times 10^9/_{16}$
(Br. 145) 4th and final state
The Library of Congress

54 The Lamp 1891
color print, with drypoint, soft-ground and
aquatint, $12^5/_8 \times 10$
(Br. 144) 3rd and final state
Mr. and Mrs. John Palmer Leeper

55 The Letter 1891
color print, with drypoint, soft-ground and
aquatint, $16 \times 11^1/_2$
(Br. 146) 3rd and final state
Mrs. Lee C. Schlesinger

56 The Fitting 1891
color print, with drypoint, soft-ground and
aquatint, $14^3/_4 \times 10^1/_8$
(Br. 147) trial proof, undescribed
The Art Institute of Chicago

57 The Fitting 1891
color print, with drypoint, soft-ground and
aquatint, $14^3/_4 \times 10^1/_8$
(Br. 147) 5th and final state
The Art Institute of Chicago

58 Mother's Kiss 1891
color print, with drypoint and aquatint,
$13^5/_8 \times 9$
(Br. 149) 5th and final state
The Library of Congress

59 Woman Bathing (also called The Toilette) 1891
color print, with drypoint and aquatint,
$14^5/_{16} \times 10^9/_{16}$
(Br. 148) 5th and final state
New York Public Library, Courtesy of the
S. P. Avery Collection. Astor, Lenox and Tilden
Foundations

60 Maternal Caress 1891
drawing for the color print (Br. 150), 14×10
Mr. and Mrs. Daniel H. Silberberg

61 Maternal Caress 1891
color print, with drypoint, soft-ground and
aquatint, $14^3/_8 \times 10^9/_{16}$
(Br. 150) 3rd and final state
The Library of Congress

62 Afternoon Tea Party 1891
color print, with drypoint and aquatint,
$13^1/_2 \times 10^1/_8$
(Br. 151) 3rd and final state
The Art Institute of Chicago

63 The Coiffure 1891
color print, with drypoint, soft-ground and
aquatint, $14^3/_8 \times 10^1/_2$
(Br. 152) 4th and final state
New York Public Library, Courtesy of the
S. P. Avery Collection. Astor, Lenox and Tilden
Foundations

64 The Banjo Lesson 1892
color print, with drypoint and aquatint,
$11^{11}/_{16} \times 9^{7}/_{16}$
(Br. 156) 4th and final state
The Library of Congress

65 Gathering Fruit (also called L'Espalier and
Le Potager) 1892
color print, with drypoint and aquatint,
$16^{3}/_{4} \times 11^{3}/_{4}$
(Br. 157) 6th and final state
Metropolitan Museum of Art, Rogers Fund

66 Feeding the Ducks 1894
color print, with drypoint and aquatint,
$11^{1}/_{2} \times 15^{1}/_{2}$
(Br. 158) undescribed state between 1st and
2nd states
Achenbach Foundation for Graphic Arts

67 Peasant Mother and Child c. 1894
color print, with drypoint and aquatint,
$12^{1}/_{2} \times 10$
(Br. 159) 5th and final state
Mrs. Gardner Cassatt

68 The Barefooted Child c. 1895
color print, with drypoint and aquatint,
$9^{7}/_{16} \times 12^{7}/_{16}$
(Br. 160) 2nd of three states
The Minneapolis Institute of Arts

69 The Barefooted Child 1895
color print, with drypoint and aquatint,
$9^{1}/_{2} \times 12^{7}/_{16}$
(Br. 160) 3rd and final state
Kovler Gallery, Chicago

70 Under the Horse Chestnut Tree c. 1895
color print, with drypoint and aquatint,
$15^{7}/_{8} \times 11^{5}/_{16}$
(Br. 162) 4th and final state
Museum of Modern Art, Gift of Abby Aldrich
Rockefeller

71 By the Pond 1895
color print, with drypoint and aquatint,
$12^{7}/_{8} \times 16^{15}/_{16}$
(Br. 161) 4th and final state
Lucas Collection: c/o Baltimore Museum of Art

72 Celeste Seated on a Park Bench c. 1899
drypoint, 11×7
(Br. 168) 2nd and final state
Philadelphia Museum of Art

73 Picking Daisies 1895
color print, with drypoint and aquatint, 13×17
undescribed 2nd state, unfinished
M. Henri M. Petiet

74 Mother Louise Nursing her Child 1899
drypoint, $13^{3}/_{16} \times 8^{15}/_{16}$
(Br. 172) 2nd and final state
The Minneapolis Institute of Arts

75 Margot and her Mother Seated on a Sofa 1901
drypoint, $16^{15}/_{16} \times 12^{7}/_{8}$
(Br. 177) only known state
Cincinnati Art Museum

76 Margot in a Floppy Bonnet Leaning Against a
Chair c. 1904
drypoint, $8^{1}/_{2} \times 5^{13}/_{16}$
(Br. 185) 1st of two states
National Gallery of Art (Rosenwald Collection)

77 Margot in a Floppy Bonnet Leaning Against a
Chair c. 1904
drypoint, $8^{1}/_{2} \times 5^{7}/_{8}$
(Br. 185) 2nd state (restrike, 1923)
Philadelphia Museum of Art

78 The Crocheting Lesson c. 1901
drypoint, $17^{5}/_{16} \times 10^{1}/_{2}$
(Br. 178) 2nd and final state
The Minneapolis Institute of Arts

79 Simone Wearing a Large Bonnet, Seated in an Armchair   c. 1904
drypoint, $9^7/_{16} \times 11^{13}/_{16}$
(Br. 192)   only known state
Philadelphia Museum of Art, William S. Pilling Collection

80 Kneeling in an Armchair   1904
drypoint, $11^7/_8 \times 9^9/_{16}$
(Br. 186)   only known state
Martin Gallery

81 Antoine Holding her Child by Both Hands 1910
drypoint, $16 \times 11^1/_4$
(Br. 208)   only known state (restrike, 1923)
Mrs. Gardner Cassatt .

82 Sara Wearing her Bonnet and Coat   c. 1904
lithograph (transfer), $20 \times 16^7/_{16}$
(Br. 198)   only known state
The Brooklyn Museum

83 Sara Wearing her Bonnet and Coat   c. 1965
facsimile of Br. 198, $20 \times 16^7/_{16}$

84 Edgar Degas
Au Louvre : La Peinture (Mary Cassatt)   c. 1880
etching, drypoint and aquatint, $11^7/_8 \times 5$
D. 29
The Brooklyn Museum

85 Au Louvre : Musée des Antiques   c. 1880
aquatint, $10^1/_2 \times 9^1/_8$ by Edgar Degas
D. 30
The Brooklyn Museum

Plates

1 Waiting. Soft-ground and aquatint

2   The Umbrella. Soft-ground on zinc.

3   The Corner of the Sofa (No. 3). Soft-ground and aquatint.

4   The Corner of the Sofa (No. 1). Drawing for soft-ground etching.

5 Two Young Ladies, Seated in a Loge, Facing Right. Soft-ground, aquatint and drypoint.

6   In the Opera Box (No. 3). Soft-ground and aquatint.

7   The Visitor. Soft-ground, aquatint and drypoint.

8   Heads of Elsie and Robert Cassatt. Drypoint.

9   Mrs. Cassatt Reading to her Grandchildren (No. 1). Soft-ground, aquatint and drypoint.

10   Woman Seated in a Loge. Lithograph on stone.

11   Lady in Black, in a Loge, Facing Right. Soft-ground and aquatint.

12   George Moore. Soft-ground and aquatint.

13 Knitting in the Glow of a Lamp. Soft-ground, aquatint and etching.

14 Knitting in the Library. Soft-ground and aquatint.

15   Lydia at Afternoon Tea. Soft-ground and aquatint.

16   Lydia and her Mother at Tea. Soft-ground and aquatint.

17 Under the Lamp. Drawing for soft-ground and aquatint.

18   Under the Lamp. Soft-ground and aquatint.

19   Before the Fireplace (No. 1). Soft-ground and aquatint.

20   Before the Fireplace (No. 2). Soft-ground and aquatint.

21   Reading the Newspaper (No. 2). Soft-ground and aquatint.

22   Mr. Cassatt Reading. Soft-ground and aquatint.

23   Mrs. Cassatt Knitting, Profile View. Soft-ground and aquatint.

24   Susan and Child Facing Each Other. Etching and drypoint.

25 Mlle. Luguet Seated on a Couch. Soft-ground and aquatint.

26   Mlle. Luguet in a Coat and Hat. Soft-ground.

27 Susan Seated before a Row of Trees. Etching and drypoint.

28   Robert Seated, Facing Left. Drypoint.

29 Solicitude. Drypoint.

30   Nurse and Baby Bill (No. 2). Soft-ground and aquatint.

31   On the Balcony. Soft-ground and aquatint.

32 A Portrait of the Artist's Mother. Soft-ground and aquatint.

33   Baby's Back. Drypoint.

34 The Map. Drypoint.

35   The Mandolin Player. Drypoint.

36　The Stocking. Drypoint.

37   Repose. Drypoint.

38 Reflection. Drypoint.

39   Tea. Drypoint.

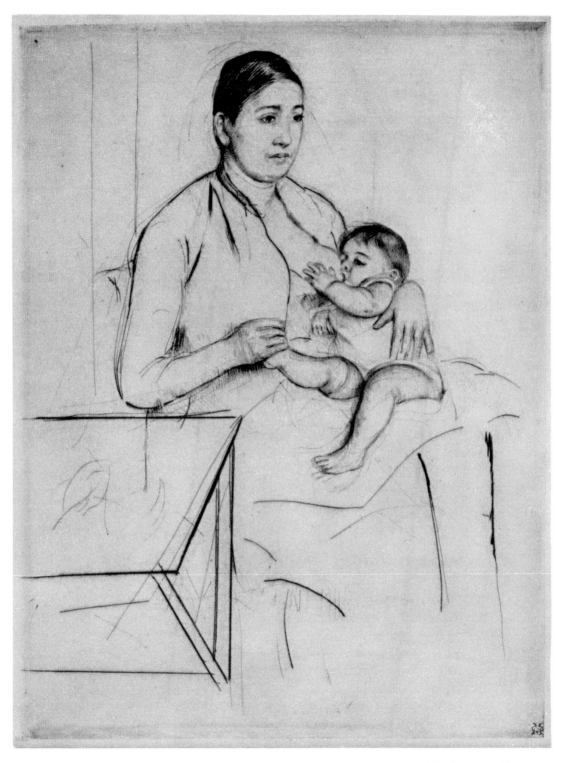

40   Nursing. Drypoint.

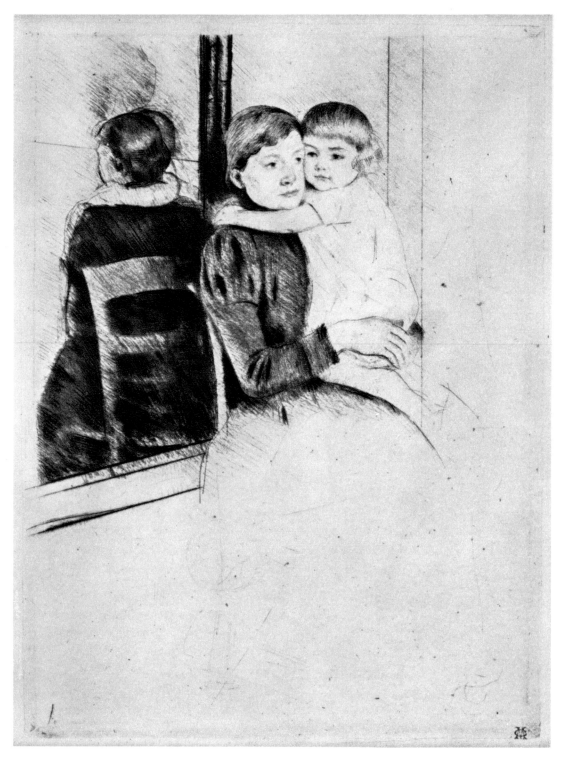

41   The Mirror. Drypoint.

42 The Bonnet. Drypoint.

43   The Parrot (third state). Drypoint.

44   The Parrot (seventh state). Drypoint.

45   Quietude. Drypoint.

46 Mrs. Gardner Cassatt and her Baby Seated Near a Window. Drypoint.

47   Gardner Held by his Mother. Drypoint.

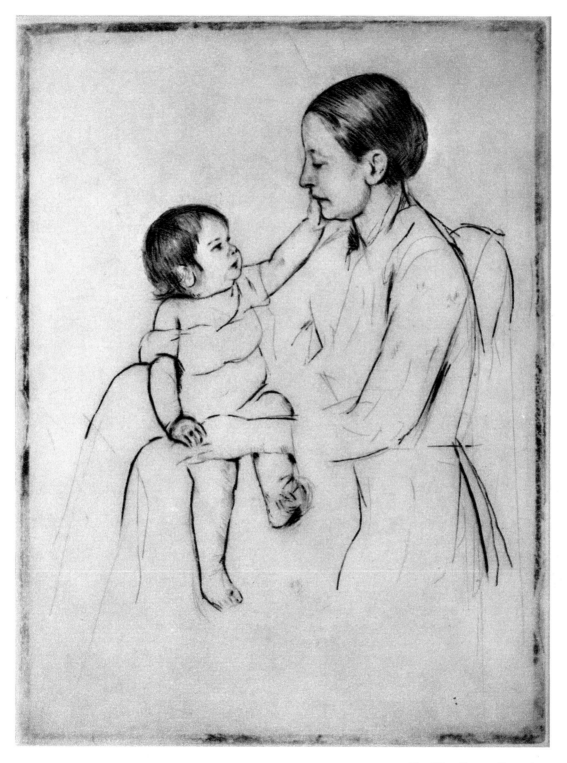

48　The Caress. Drypoint.

49 The Bath (fifth state). Color print, with drypoint, soft-ground and aquatint.

52   The Bath (eleventh state). Color print, with drypoint, soft-ground and aquatint.

53 In the Omnibus. Color print, with drypoint, soft-ground and aquatint.

54   The Lamp. Color print, with drypoint, soft-ground and aquatint.

55   The Letter. Color print, with drypoint, soft-ground and aquatint.

56   The Fitting. Color print, with drypoint, soft-ground and aquatint.

58   Mother's Kiss. Color print, with drypoint and aquatint.

59   Woman Bathing. Color print, with drypoint and aquatint.

60   Maternal Caress. Drawing for color print.

61 Maternal Caress. Color print, with drypoint, soft-ground and aquatint.

62 Afternoon Tea Party. Color print, with drypoint and aquatint.

63   The Coiffure. Color print, with drypoint, soft-ground and aquatint.

64 The Banjo Lesson. Color print, with drypoint and aquatint.

65 Gathering Fruit. Color print, with drypoint and aquatint.

66   Feeding the Ducks. Color print, with drypoint and aquatint.

67 Peasant Mother and Child. Color print, with drypoint and aquatint.

68   The Barefooted Child (second state). Color print, with drypoint and aquatint.

69   The Barefooted Child (third state). Color print, with drypoint and aquatint.

70   Under the Horse Chestnut Tree. Color print, with drypoint and aquatint.

71   By the Pond. Color print, with drypoint and aquatint.

72 Celeste Seated on a Park Bench. Drypoint.

73   Picking Daisies. Color print, with drypoint and aquatint.

74　Mother Louise Nursing her Child. Drypoint.

75   Margot and her Mother Seated on a Sofa. Drypoint.

77   Margot in a Floppy Bonnet Leaning against a Chair. Drypoint.

78   The Crocheting Lesson. Drypoint.

79 Simone Wearing a Large Bonnet, Seated in Armchair. Drypoint.

80 Kneeling in an Armchair. Drypoint.

81 Antoine Holding her Child by Both Hands. Drypoint.

82   Sara Wearing Bonnet and Coat. Lithograph.

85 Au Louvre: Musée des Antiques. Aquatint by Edgar Degas.

Selected Bibliography

Books

Breeskin, Adelyn D. *The Graphic Work of Mary Cassatt.* H. Bittner & Co., New York, 1948.

Bruening, Margaret. *Mary Cassatt.* Hyperion Press, New York, 1944.

Carson, Julia M. H. *Mary Cassatt.* David McKay Co., New York, 1966.

Segard, Achille. *Un Peintre des Enfants et des Mères—Mary Cassatt.* Librairie Ollendorf, Paris, 1913.

Sweet, Frederick A. *Miss Mary Cassatt/Impressionist from Pennsylvania.* University of Oklahoma Press, Norman, Oklahoma, 1966.

Valerie, Edith. *Mary Cassatt.* Crès & Cie, Paris, 1930.

Watson, Forbes. *Mary Cassatt.* American Artists Series: Whitney Museum of American Art, New York, 1932.

Magazine Articles

Alexandre, Arsène. "La Collection Havemeyer et Miss Cassatt." *La Renaissance de l'Art*, tome 13, Février, 1930, pp. 51–56.

Alexandre, Arsène. "Miss Mary Cassatt aquafortiste." *La Renaissance de l'Art*, tome 7, Mars, 1924, pp. 127–133.

Biddle, George. "Some Memories of Mary Cassatt." *The Arts*, August, 1926, vol. 10, pp. 107–111.

Brinton, Christian. "Concerning Miss Cassatt and Certain Etchings." *International Studio*, Feb., 1916, vol. 27, pp. I–VI.

Carey, Elizabeth Luther. "The Art of Mary Cassatt." *The Scrip*, New York, Oct., 1905, vol. I, no. 1, pp. 1–5.

Denoinville, Georges. "Mary Cassatt Peintre des Enfants et des Mères." *Byblis*, Hiver, 1928, pp. 121–123.

Fuller, Sue. "Mary Cassatt's Use of Soft-ground Etching." *Magazine of Art*, Feb., 1950, no. 43, pp. 54–57.

Geffroy, Gustave. "Femmes Artistes—Un Peintre de l'Enfance: Mary Cassatt." *Les Modes*, vol. 4, Février, 1904, pp. 4–11.

Grafly, Dorothy. "In Retrospect—Mary Cassatt." *American Magazine of Art*, June, 1927, vol. 18, pp. 305–312.

Havemeyer, Louisine W. "The Cassatt Exhibition." *Pennsylvania Museum Bulletin*, no. 113, vol. 22, May, 1927, pp. 373–382.

Hyslop, Francis E., Jr., "Berthe Morisot and Mary Cassatt." *College Art Journal*, Spring, 1954, vol. XIII, no. 3, pp. 179–184.

Ivins, William M., Jr. *Bulletin of the Metropolitan Museum of Art*, Jan., 1927, vol. XXII, no. 1, pp. 9 and 10.

Johnson, Una E. "The Graphic Art of Mary Cassatt." *American Artist*, Nov., 1945, vol. 9, no. 9, pp. 18–21.

Mauclair, Camille. "Un Peintre de l'Enfance: Mary Cassatt." *L'Art Décoratif*, tome IV, no. 47, Août, 1902, pp. 177–185.

McChesney, Clara. "Mary Cassatt and Her Work." *Arts and Decorations*, June, 1913, vol. 3, pp. 265–267.

Mellerio, André. "Mary Cassatt." *L'Art et Les Artistes*, Nov., 1910, tome 12, pp. 69–75.

Newman, Gemma. "Greatness of Mary Cassatt." *American Artist*, Feb., 1966, vol. 30, pp. 42–49, 64–65.

Pica, Vittorio. "Artisti Contemporanei—Berthe Morisot e Mary Cassatt." *Emporium*, Bergamo, Jan., 1907, vol 26, no. 3, pp. 11–16.

Preston, S. "Paintings at Knoedler's." *Apollo*, April, 1966, vol. 83, pp. 303–304.

"Realists and Mystics, 1860–1900." *Art in America*, Aug., 1965, vol. 53, pp. 62–65.

Richardson, E. P. "Sophisticates and Innocents Abroad." *Art News*, April, 1954, pp. 20–23.

Smith, D. L. "Observations on a Few Celebrated Women Artists." *American Artist*, Jan., 1962, vol. 26, pp. 78–81.

Spencer, Eleanor P. "Modern Look through Impressionist Eyes." *Art News*, April, 1962, vol. 61, pp. 29–31, 55–56.

Sweet, Frederick A. "America's Greatest Woman Painter." *Vogue*, Feb., 1954, vol. 123, no. 3, pp. 102–103.

Tabarant, Adolph. "Les Disparus—Miss Mary Cassatt." *Bulletin de la Vie Artistique*, Juillet, 1926, pp. 205–206.

Teal, Gardner. "Mother & Child—The Theme as Developed in the Art of Mary Cassatt." *Good Housekeeping*, vol. 50, Feb., 1910, pp. 141–146.

Walker, John. "Mary Cassatt." *Ladies Home Journal*, July, 1947, vol. LXIV, no. 7. p. 40.

Walter, William. "Miss Mary Cassatt." *Scribner's* vol. XIX, no. 3, March, 1896, pp. 353–361.

Watson, Forbes. "Philadelphia Pays Tribute to Mary Cassatt." *The Arts*, June, 1927, vol. 11, pp. 289–297.

Weitenkampf, Frank. "The Drypoints of Mary Cassatt." *Print Collector's Quarterly*, vol. VI, Dec., 1916, pp. 397–409.

Welch, M. L. "Mary Cassatt." *American Society Legion of Honor Magazine*, Summer, 1954, pp. 155–165.

Selected Introductions to Exhibition Catalogues

Baltimore Museum of Art. A Comprehensive Exhibition of the Work of Mary Cassatt, 1941.

Leeper, J. P., Jr. Exhibition at the Pasadena Art Institute, "Mary Cassatt and her Parisian Friends," 1951.

Mellerio, André. Préface de Exposition Mary Cassatt chez Durand-Ruel en 1893.

Sweet, F. A. "Sargent, Whistler and Mary Cassatt." Exhibition at the Art Institute of Chicago and the Metropolitan Museum, 1954.

Wildenstein and Company, New York. Exhibition of the Works of Mary Cassatt, 1947.

This book was set in Walbaum type
by Brüder Rosenbaum of Vienna, Austria,
printed in monogravure and color offset
by Amilcare Pizzi S. p. A. of Milano, Italy.
Design by Ulrich Ruchti.